KU-104-362

# A PORTRAIT OF
# CARDIFF

For Delyth, Rebecca and Emily

# A PORTRAIT OF
# CARDIFF

GERAINT TELLEM

HALSGROVE

First published in Great Britain in 2004

Copyright © 2004 text and photographs Geraint Tellem

Title page: The Clock Tower, Cardiff Castle

*All rights reserved. No part of this publication may be reproduced, stored in a retrieval system, or transmitted in any form or by any means without the prior permission of the copyright holder.*

**British Library Cataloguing-in-Publication Data**
A CIP record for this title is available from the British Library


ISBN 1 84114 377 4


**HALSGROVE**
Halsgrove House
Lower Moor Way
Tiverton, Devon EX16 6SS
Tel: 01884 243242
Fax: 01884 243325
email: sales@halsgrove.com
website: www.halsgrove.com


Printed and bound by D'Auria Industrie Grafiche Spa, Italy

# Introduction

Until the beginning of the nineteenth century, Cardiff was a relatively insignificant township. It originated on the site of a Roman fort, built at the mouths of the Rivers Taff and Ely in about 75AD. The name 'Cardiff' is probably derived from 'Caer Taf' (Taff Fort) or 'Caer Didi' (Didius's Fort, referring to the Roman general Aulua Didius). After the decline of Roman civilisation in the fourth century, the site remained more or less unoccupied until the Norman Conquest. In the twelfth century the wooden castle was rebuilt in stone, and a market town grew up around it.

In 1404, Cardiff was sacked by Owain Glyndwr but was quickly re-established. The 1536 Act of Union brought a measure of stability, but the population remained static until around 1800. Ultimately, its coastal location and close proximity to the coalfields of the valleys to the north led to Cardiff's emergence as one of the world's busiest ports and subsequently to the vibrant, cosmopolitan city that exists today.

During the late eighteenth century, Wales was transformed by the Industrial Revolution and the production of iron and coal increased at a phenomenal rate. In 1766, the Bute family arrived in Cardiff, acquiring vast estates and mineral rights. They were to play a pivotal role in Cardiff's history, opening the first docks, the Glamorganshire Canal, and the Taff Vale Railway. Such was their influence, that the second Marquess became known as the creator of modern Cardiff. Their contribution to the burgeoning iron and coal industry culminated in 1913, with over 10 million tons of coal being exported through the Butetown docks, securing Cardiff's position as the world's premier coal exporting port.

The Butes continued to open more docks such as the East Dock in 1855, Roath Basin in 1874 and Roath Dock in 1887 and a multi-cultural community known as Tiger Bay grew up around them. The population increased dramatically, reaching 170,000 by the end of the century and 227,000 by 1931. In 1905, Cardiff was designated as a city and at this time, the elegant Civic Centre was created. The Coal Exchange in Mount Stuart Square became the centre of commerce, trading with the London Stock Exchange and dictating the price of coal on world markets.

After the First World War, coal production declined and the city was badly affected by the Great Depression of the 1930s. German bombing during the Second World War claimed over 350 lives, and large parts of Butetown were destroyed. The docklands continued to decline drastically, but large areas of the city were rebuilt.

Cardiff was made capital of Wales in 1955. This heralded the birth of the modern city and today there is no doubt about its position at the heart of Welsh affairs. Not only the seat of the Welsh government, but most of the country's industry and commerce are concentrated here and the city has a rich architectural heritage, also boasting large areas of parks and gardens. Cardiff Castle occupies a prominent position in the city centre, which features some of the best shopping facilities in the country, notable for the Victorian and Edwardian arcades. The Wales Millennium Stadium has established itself as a focal point for British sport as well as being the home of Welsh rugby. It is one of the most futuristic structures in the UK and is seen by many as a symbol of the dynamic changes that have taken place in Cardiff over the last twenty years. These changes look set to continue on a large scale well into the twenty-first century.

In 1987, the Cardiff Bay Development Corporation was formed, instigating the docklands rejuvenation that is still in progress today. Massive investment has completely transformed the area. The Cardiff Barrage has created a 500-acre freshwater lake, around which a vast amount of development has taken place. The National Assembly of Wales and the Cardiff Council Headquarters are located here, accompanied by luxurious waterfront apartment blocks, prestigious corporate offices and thriving restaurant quarters. At the time of writing, the Wales Millennium Centre, destined to be one of the country's most important cultural arenas, is nearing completion.

Cardiff was, in fact, one of three ports in the area to develop as a result of coal; the other two being Penarth, at the western end of Cardiff Bay, and Barry, a few miles further down the coast. Penarth is famous for its huge Victorian pier and became known as the 'Garden by the Sea' because of its beautiful parks and gardens. The old dock has now been converted into a large marina.

Situated 2 miles north-west of the city, Llandaff Cathedral stands on the site of a sixth century church founded by St Teilo. The present cathedral was begun in the twelfth century and completed by the fifteenth century. Practically every style of medieval architecture is found here. After suffering serious neglect in the middle ages, it was restored in the nineteenth century, but severely damaged by a German landmine in 1941. Major rebuilding took place after the war, when the Welch Regiment Chapel was added, along with Sir Jacob Epstein's sculpture 'Christ in Majesty'. The mismatched western towers are evidence of the different styles adopted over the centuries. The northwest tower is by Jasper Tudor dating from the fifteenth century, while the adjoining tower and spire were rebuilt from nineteenth century designs.

The countryside around Cardiff is as diverse as the city itself. To the south-west, a spectacular coastline of limestone cliffs and sandy beaches gives way to the gently undulating landscape of the Vale of Glamorgan, with its picturesque villages and market towns. Immediately to the north lie the mountains and valleys that were at the centre of the Welsh coal industry and these eventually merge with the spectacular windblown landscape of the Brecon Beacons National Park.

My principal aim in compiling this book has been to try and portray the many different aspects of Cardiff whilst taking a brief glimpse at the surrounding area. Most of the photographs were taken between September 2003 and June 2004. I have tried to keep the material as up to date as possible, but the sheer pace of development in certain areas has made this extremely difficult! Nevertheless, I hope that what follows will, to a certain extent, illustrate why Cardiff is now regarded as one of the world's most exciting young capitals.

*Geraint Tellem*
*June 2004*

# Acknowledgements

I would like to thank a number of people who have helped me during the preparation of this book:

First and foremost, my wife Delyth and family who have given me continued encouragement and support.

Special thanks go to Ceri-Anne Sullock at Cardiff City Centre Management; Jennifer Andrews at Cardiff County Council; the staff of City Hall, Cardiff; Claire Hamer and Kevin Burt at Cardiff Castle; The Dean and Chapter of Llandaff Cathedral; Helen Lowcock James at the Museum of Welsh Life; Gwyn Sobey at Urban City; John Michell at King Sturge, Capital Tower.

I acknowledge with thanks the assistance of many other people, companies and institutions, who have made this book possible.

# Contents

Central Cardiff

**Cardiff City Hall**
Completed 1904, officially opened 1905, it is the centrepiece of the Civic Centre.

**Cardiff City Hall**
The design is based on English and French Renaissance models and built of Portland Stone. The pool and fountains were constructed in 1969 to commemorate the investiture of Prince Charles as Prince of Wales.

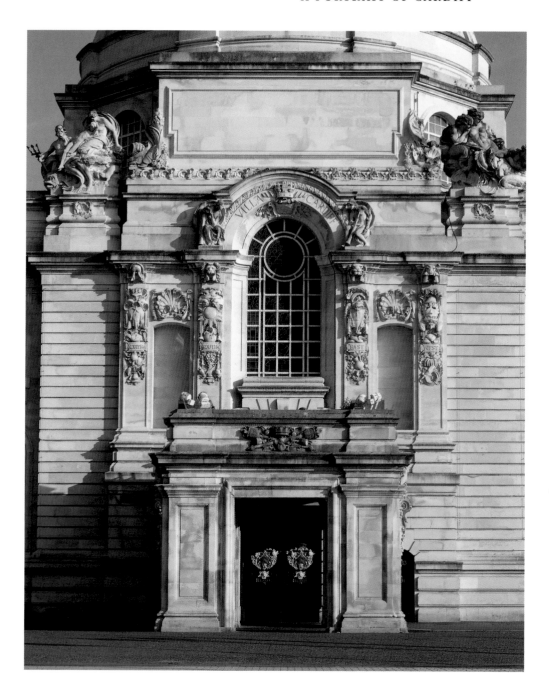

**Cardiff City Hall – main entrance**
Above the portico the statues
represent the sea receiving the
city's three rivers: the Taff, the Ely
and the Rhymney.

**Cardiff City Hall**
The stained glass window in the Council Chamber
depicts the commercial life of the Principality.

**Cardiff City Hall**
The dome with its fierce Welsh Dragon.

**Cardiff City Hall**
The clock tower is 194ft high and
the statues represent the four winds.

**City Hall from Alexandra Gardens**
The minutes and hours of the skeleton clock are gilt with English Gold Leaf. A bell strikes on the hour and the Westminster Quarter Chimes are chimed on four-quarter bells.

**A Civic Christmas**
Every Christmas, a fairground and
ice rink provide entertainment
outside the City Hall.

**Cardiff City Hall – the Marble Hall**
Lined with columns of Sienna Marble, the Marble Hall displays many items from the city's extensive art collection.

**Entrance to the National Museum and Gallery**
One of Britain's finest museums, featuring the Evolution of Wales Gallery,
Natural History galleries and extensive art galleries.

**Cardiff Civic Centre**
Three buildings – the Law Courts, the
City Hall and the National Museum and
Gallery of Wales, front this. They enclose
a large rectangle within which tree-lined
avenues bisect Cathays Park.

**The Welsh National War Memorial, Alexandra Gardens**
This was completed in 1928 to commemorate soldiers who died in the First World War.
A plaque for those who died in the Second World War was added in 1949.

**War Memorial**
The Memorial is the focus of the annual Remembrance Day Parade in November.

**Main Building, Cardiff University**
The University was established in 1883 and is one of Britain's most successful research and teaching universities.

**Entrance to Main Building, Cardiff University**
The University has some 13,000 undergraduate and 3000 postgraduate students studying science, engineering, humanities and business courses.

**Lloyd George Statue, Civic Centre**
David Lloyd George (1863 – 1945)
was the British Prime Minister
from 1916 to 1922 and one of the
most successful politicians in
Welsh history.

**St David's Hall**
Opened in 1983, this is the national
concert hall of Wales with over 450
performances a year covering classical
music, rock/pop concerts, jazz,
children's events, dance and comedy.

### St David's Hall

St David's Hall has one of the best acoustic auditoriums in Europe and is the main concert venue for the BBC National Orchestra of Wales.

**St John's Church**
The church is one of the oldest medieval buildings in Cardiff and dates from the twelfth century.

**Castle Arcade**
Often regarded as the prettiest, this arcade was built in 1887 and hosts some excellent clothing shops and cafés.

Castle Arcade

**Morgan Arcade**
Built in 1896, the arcade features
Venetian windows on the first floor
with several units boasting original
wooden shop fronts.

**High Street Arcade**
This arcade is noted for its clothes shops and dates from 1886. It runs from the High Street to St John's Square.

**Queen Street**
The statue of Aneurin Bevan (1897-1960),
post-war politician and founder of the National Health Service,
dominates the western end of Queen Street.

**Venetian shopping façade, Queen Street**
Built in 1870, this is an example of the fine nineteenth-century architecture in the area.

**Capitol Shopping Centre**
Situated at the eastern end of
Queen Street, this has been
completely refurbished and is
one of the most important retail
outlets in the city centre.

Queen Street at night

**Queens Arcade shopping centre**
Situated in the heart of Cardiff,
comprising around 50 stores.

Queens Arcade shopping centre

**Cardiff Market**
Built out of riveted cast iron and glass, the market is on two storeys.

**Cardiff Market**
The large indoor market built in 1891, sells a wide variety of goods such as fish,
meat, fruit and cheese as well as pets, electronics, and second-hand records.

The Old Arcade Pub,
Church Street

**Brains Pub window**
There are over 200 Brains Pubs across Wales and the company, founded by Samuel Arthur Brain in 1882, is now Wales's leading drinks and hospitality company.

**New Theatre**
This Edwardian theatre is the premier theatre in Wales and presents a wide range of performances: opera, ballet, musical theatre, drama and pantomime.

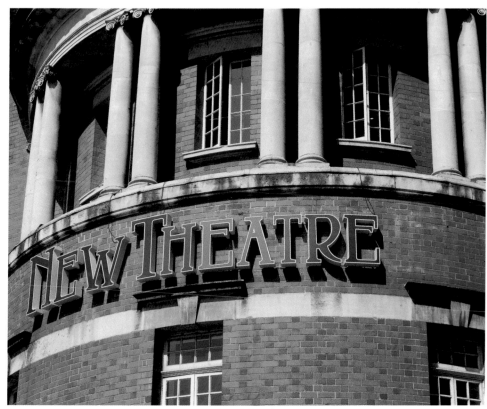

New Theatre

**The Norman Keep, Cardiff Castle**
Originally a Roman fort, it was
rebuilt by the Normans. In 1865,
the Third Marquess of Bute
appointed William Burges to
undertake a major restoration,
completed by 1872.

The Norman Keep, Cardiff Castle

**Clock Tower, Cardiff Castle**
Built between 1869 and 1872 this
contained a series of 'medieval'
bachelor apartments for the young
marquess with summer and winter
smoking rooms and a bedroom
complete with Roman bath.

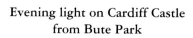

Evening light on Cardiff Castle
from Bute Park

**Cardiff Castle**
The turrets and towers of the castle's domestic buildings merge with the modern outline of the Millennium Stadium in this view from the Keep.

Bute Park in autumn

**Millennium Stadium**
Built at a cost of around £130 million, the Millennium Stadium has a capacity of 72,500.

**Millennium Stadium**
The new stadium has replaced Cardiff Arms Park as the home of Welsh rugby and hosted the Rugby World Cup in 1999, the year of its inauguration.

**Millennium Stadium**
On the western side, the walkways
are cantilevered over the adjacent
River Taff.

Looking down the Taff towards the Millennium Stadium

**Evening light on the Millennium Stadium**
The real grass turf is grown on thousands of pallets, which can be removed for large-scale concerts.

**Star Century Cinema and Millennium Stadium at dusk**

**Stadium Supplies**
The stadium has seven restaurants
and 22 public bars.

The Taff and Millennium Stadium at night

Looking south-west over central Cardiff

**Mill Lane**
Cardiff has a wide range of restaurants, many of which are
concentrated in the 'Café Quarter' around Mill Lane.

**The Taff Trail**
Running for 68 miles, the Taff Trail
links Cardiff Bay and Brecon using
old railway lines, canals and forestry
paths along the Taff valley via
Pontypridd and Merthyr Tydfil.

The Taff Trail in autumn

**Roath Park**

This Victorian park covers 130 acres and the dam creating the lake was completed in 1891.
The lighthouse is a memorial to the Scott expedition of 1910–12 *(see page 91)*.

Cardiff Bay

**Pierhead Building**
Dominating the waterfront at Cardiff Bay, this was opened in 1897.

### Pierhead Building
Built of brick and terracotta, it was initially the headquarters of the Cardiff Municipal Railway Company (formerly the Bute Docks Company). It is currently an exhibition centre giving information about the Welsh Assembly.

The Pierhead Building and Mermaid Quay, Cardiff Bay

**Mermaid Quay**
This consists of a vibrant mix of restaurants, bars and cafés as well as sophisticated shops
and services. Its architecture is inspired by the maritime location.

**Lightship 2000**
This was constructed in Dartmouth in 1953 and spent much of her time as the Helwick light on the Gower peninsula. It now serves as a centre for Christian friendship in Cardiff Bay.

**Waterfront at Roath Basin, Cardiff Bay**
Roath Basin was constructed in the latter part of the nineteenth century. The area decayed during
the twentieth century, although in recent years massive regeneration has taken place.

**Cardiff Barrage**
The controversial construction of the Cardiff Bay Barrage – built across the Ely and Taff estuaries and completed
in 1999 – has transformed a vast mudflat into a 500-acre freshwater lake with 8 miles of waterfront.

**Cardiff Barrage**
The effect of the tide (with a range of up to 14ft) has been eliminated by the
barrage and a vast variety of new building has taken place around the bay,
including the new Wales Millennium Centre.

Looking towards Penarth across Cardiff Bay

Cardiff Bay

**Atradius Building**
This was opened in 1995. The maritime setting overlooking the bay inspired the design.

**Atradius Building**
It is generally regarded as one of the most exciting buildings built in Wales over the past half-century.

**Techniquest**
This is the UK's leading Science Discovery Centre with 160 hands-on exhibits.
There is a Planetarium, a Lab, a Discovery Centre and a high-tech Science Theatre.

The National Assembly for Wales Building, Cardiff Bay

**County Hall**
Situated in Atlantic Wharf, this features an innovative 'pagoda' style with a Welsh slate roof.

**Roald Dahl Plas**
**(formerly the Oval Basin)**
Originally an old lock, it was filled
in during the 1960s and has been
designed for open-air performances.

**Wales Millennium Centre**
Designed as one of the country's principal performance venues for opera, ballet, dance and musicals.

**Wales Millennium Centre**
Wales has a strong Romano-Celtic heritage and
the inscription is based on classical and pagan
traditions. It reads as follows:

'Creu Gwir Fel Gwydr O Ffwrnais Awen/
In These Stones Horizons Sing.'

The Welsh inscription translates as 'creating
truth like glass from the furnace of inspiration'.
It was composed by the poet Gwyneth Jones.

Water sculpture and Wales
Millennium Centre, Cardiff Bay

**Atlantic Wharf Leisure Village**
Described as 'offering the complete leisure experience under one roof', it contains a 12-screen cinema, 26-lane Hollywood Bowl, as well as bars, restaurants and a nightclub.

Modern housing development near Roath Basin, Cardiff Bay

Residential apartments, Cardiff Bay

**St David's Hotel**
This hotel creates a striking landmark across Cardiff Bay. It is the first purpose-built five-star hotel in Wales.

**Scott Memorial, Cardiff Bay**
Captain Scott sailed in the *Terra Nova* from Cardiff in June 1910 on the ill-fated expedition to the South Pole.

**Norwegian Church**
Built as a seamen's chapel in 1868,
it was dismantled in 1987 and
re-erected on the present site as the
Norwegian Church Arts Centre.

# Llandaff Cathedral

Llandaff Cathedral from the east in autumn

Llandaff Cathedral interior from the west door

Epstein's statue 'Christ in Majesty'

West front (c.1220)
Llandaff Cathedral

Llandaff Cathedral from the
south-west featuring the
Pritchard Spire of 1869

The thirteeth-century
Chapter House

War Memorial and Llandaff Cathedral

Lady Chapel, Llandaff Cathedral

The Taff and Llandaff
Cathedral at sunrise

**Bishop's Castle, Llandaff**
Probably constructed by Bishop William de Braose after 1266, it was ruined by Owain Glyndwr in 1404.

# Cardiff and Environs

**Parc Cefn Onn**
Situated to the north of Cardiff,
this is notable for its striking
autumn colours and brilliant
displays of rhododendron and
azaleas in early summer.

**Kennixton Farmhouse, Museum of Welsh Life**
Built 1610, re-erected 1955, this is a typical farmhouse from the Gower in south-west Wales.

**St Fagans Castle, Museum of Welsh Life**
One of the finest Elizabethan manor houses in Wales, begun in 1580,
and completed in 1620. A major refurbishment took place in 1850.

**Cilewent Farmhouse, Museum of Welsh Life**
Built 1470, rebuilt 1734, re-erected 1959. Known as a longhouse, with cattle at one end and their owners at the other.

**Rhyd-y Car Ironworkers' Houses, Museum of Welsh Life**
Built in 1800 for ironworkers in Merthyr Tydfil they were re-erected in 1987 and display
different periods of their history – 1805, 1855, 1895, 1925, 1955 and 1985.

### Castell Coch

William Burges, the designer of Cardiff Castle, built this for the third Marquess of Bute in 1875. Although it has an authentic medieval look, the interiors have been described as 'pure Victorian fantasy'.

Castell Coch from the
golf course, Tongwynlais

**Looking towards Cardiff from
Gwaelod-y-Garth**
The hills immediately north of
Cardiff offer panoramic views of the
city and the surrounding area.

**Evening light over Cardiff Bay from Penarth**

Storm clouds gather over Penarth Pier

**View over the Bristol Channel
from Penarth Pier**
The islands of Steep Holm and
Flat Holm can be seen on the horizon.

**Penarth Pier**
Originally built of cast iron with a timber deck, the 650ft pier opened in 1895. The pavilion was added in the 1920s.

**Penarth Pier**
Steamer traffic has always been the mainstay of the pier.
It was fully restored during the 1990s.

The promenade and
pier, Penarth

The Custom House,
Penarth Marina

**The Marina, Penarth**
This is situated within the sheltered waters of Cardiff Bay
and built around the basins of the historic Penarth Docks.

The Marina, Penarth

**Caerphilly Castle at sunrise**
Begun in 1268, the Castle took fifty-eight years to complete.  It is famous for its
broken tower which is the result of subsidence rather than battle.

**Caerphilly Castle**
This is the largest castle in Wales and was restored in the 1930s by the fourth Marquess of Bute.

**Caerphilly Castle**
It was one of the first to use concentric fortifications and lakes for defence.

**Dyffryn Gardens**
The Dyffryn estate dates back to the seventh century A.D. Each garden or 'outdoor room'
is enclosed within clipped yew hedges and has its own distinct character.

**Dyffryn Gardens**
The country house was built as the family residence of John Cory in 1893 and Thomas Mawson designed the gardens in 1906.

The mansion at Dyffryn

Sculpture – Dyffryn Gardens

**Rhondda Heritage Park**
Based at the former Lewis Merthyr Colliery, Trehafod, which closed in 1983, the exhibitions
here explain what life was like for miners and their families.

**Looking towards Treorchy, Rhondda Fawr**
At the beginning of the twentieth century, the Rhondda valleys were
among the most important coal mining areas in the world.

**Ferndale, Rhondda Fach**
The last coal to be produced in
the Rhondda was brought to the
surface in June 1986.

**Looking towards Pen-y-Fan, Brecon Beacons National Park**
At 886 metres (2907ft), Pen-y-Fan is the highest point in South Wales.

Sgwd Isaf Clun Gwyn waterfall, Ystradfellte, Brecon Beacons National Park

**Ogmore Castle**
The castle was begun by Maurice de Londres in 1128,
but the Keep was added in the thirteenth century.

**Ogmore Castle**
The castle is situated beside the River Ogmore, and the stepping stones, built around
the same time as the castle, lead to the picturesque village of Merthyr Mawr.

**Thatched cottage, Merthyr Mawr**
A narrow lane leads into this tiny village of thatched cottages,
before continuing to some of the highest sand dunes in Europe.

**St Hilary Church, near Cowbridge**
The Vale of Glamorgan contains numerous villages surrounded by rich pastoral land.
This church is typical of a number in the area.

**Glamorgan Heritage Coast**
This stretches for 14 miles from west Aberthaw to Porthcawl. It is noted
for its spectacular limestone cliffs and sandy beaches.

Dunraven Bay, Southerndown,
Vale of Glamorgan

Near Nash Point

**Nash Point** *(right)*

**Nash Point Lighthouse** *(below)*
This was built in 1832 to mark the sandbanks in the Bristol Channel. It was the last manned light-house in Wales, not automated until 1998.

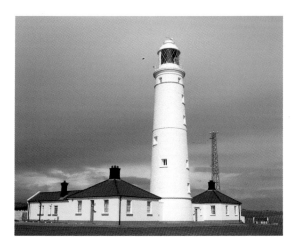

**Sunset over the Bristol Channel near Nash Point**
The channel has the second highest tidal range in the world –
second only to the Bay of Fundy in Nova Scotia, Canada.